MW01031683

ACTION

Other Books by
DR. DAVID GRIFFIN

In Honor of The Charleston 9:
A Study of Change Following Tragedy

ACTION

9 MISSIONS FOR PERSONAL AND PROFESSIONAL GROWTH

DR. DAVID GRIFFIN

TABLE OF CONTENTS

FOR THE CHARLESTON 9; FIREFIGHTERS
WHO LOST THEIR LIVES ON JUNE 18, 2007
IN CHARLESTON, SOUTH CAROLINA, WHILE
BATTLING A COMMERCIAL STRUCTURE FIRE.
REST IN PEACE.

Captain Mike Benke
Captain Billy Hutchinson
Captain Louis Mulkey
Engineer Mark Kelsey
Engineer Brad Baity
Assistant Engineer Michael French
Firefighter James Earl Drayton
Firefighter Melvin Champaign
Firefighter Brandon Thompson

Melissa:

I love you with all of my heart, forever and always.

AUTHOR'S NOTE

I learned from my own experiences how a lack of change and progression can lead to a tragedy. I am a firefighter by trade in Charleston, South Carolina where I once embraced a culture of "the way we've always done it." Being born in Charleston and a graduate of The Citadel, The Military College of South Carolina, I was deeply rooted in this belief due to the rich history and tradition of the area.

After a few years in the fire service in Charleston, I responded to an incident on June 18, 2007 as the operator of the first due engine where 9 of my fellow firefighters lost their lives. This did not occur because the fire was a perfect storm of events. This occurred due to a lack of change and progression within myself and my organization. We were ingrained in the belief of operating the way we always had and unfortunately, did not have the desire to change.

Personally, even after 9 of my fellow firefighters perished in this commercial structure fire, I continued to resist change as I thought it would make me soft. During my resistance, I realized that many of the actions I performed as the pump operator that fateful day in 2007 were outdated and did not follow national best practices. Meaning that, many of the 9 firefighters who perished did so on the hose lines that I was operating in this antiquated manner. That's something I live with every day. However, it has given me new direction and a passion to ensure people all over the world understand how important change and progression are, both personally and professionally.

So how does this relate to you? It doesn't matter whether you're a firefighter, a doctor, a lawyer, a business professional, a teacher, etc. We all encounter changes that we struggle with. It happens for many reasons. However, we must identify the components of our resistance and take positive steps to overcome them. This involves changing the hearts and minds of people whose beliefs are deeply ingrained. Needless to say, the change will be difficult, but in the end, worthwhile.

This book includes 9 missions for your personal and professional growth. Why 9 do you ask? Well at this point, I don't think I have to explain the significance the number 9 has in my life. Also, in our fast paced society, people are looking for something short, sweet, and to the point in their learning process. I've read numerous books with daily motivational stories; however, I became overwhelmed because each day gave me something new to improve upon, when I hadn't yet mastered the previous day's objective. I was getting a lot of ideas, but I wasn't able to focus on them long enough. Therefore, I envisioned a book that included 9 missions for personal and professional growth that one could utilize daily, monthly, or yearly. That way, the necessary time could be devoted to complete each mission, allowing for more growth at all levels

As in the military, tactical patience is important on all types of missions. It's no different than the journey that you're about to embark upon. You can read this book in one sitting to provoke a great deal of thought, you can utilize it over time in your business to motivate your employees, or you can complete it one mission at a time. The framework is there for you to utilize it how you may so that you can embrace change, which in turn, will allow you to have a positive impact on the hearts and minds of others around you.

As I previously explained, I resisted change at the core of my being, even to the point where I gained support from other firefighters. However, with a new found love for education, I realized that *I* was the one that needed to change. Unfortunately, it took many years of deep self-exploration, alcohol abuse, prescription drug abuse, mixed martial arts fighting, and finally, the lowest point of my life, before I came to this realization. I was hanging on to the past; hanging on to a culture that took away 9 firefighters, 9 fathers, 9 sons, 9 brothers, 9 uncles, and 9 of my friends. It's sad that it takes a tragedy for a culture to wake up and make positive change.

My challenge to you is this: take these 9 missions and embrace them both personally and professionally. As I said, it doesn't matter your profession. I have been fortunate enough to speak internationally at hundreds of organizations, universities, and professional conferences where I hear the same comment constantly; "We have people here that say that's the way we've always done it". It's now up to you to change this thought process in yourself, your family, your co-workers, and your organization. If you don't, eventually it will catch up to you. Your stocks will fall, your profit margins will drop, or it could cost someone their life.

Take it from me. Don't wait until an event provokes change, as it will haunt you for the rest of your days. Take ACTION now with these 9 missions. They *will* change your life. I know this, because they changed mine.

—*Griff*

MISSION 1

THROUGH LEARNING

*"Through learning, we re-create ourselves.
Through learning, we become able to do something
we never were able to do. Through learning, we
re-perceive the world and our relationship to it.
Through learning, we extend our capacity to create,
to be part of the generative process of life."*

—Peter M. Senge: author,
learning organization expert, and
senior lecturer at MIT.

Learning is not only essential for our individual success, but also for the quality of work we perform. More than likely you've been talking to that little voice inside your head about the changes occurring in your organization or profession. You've probably even had arguments with it just to make sure you're staying true to "the way you've always done it." What you must remember is that "the way you've always done it" does not necessarily mean that's the way it should be done in today's innovative world. Essentially, if you're making that detrimental statement, it's time to change.

Now this will not be an easy process. It will include changing your heart and mind to believe in something different than "the way you've always done it." That's a difficult undertaking. It's even more difficult when a leader is the one that does not want to change. Are you that leader? I sure hope not because if so, you're holding your employees and your organization back from success.

So, how do you change your heart and mind when they have become entrenched with specific beliefs? First, you must examine the change and understand why it's bothering you. Is it because the change wasn't your idea? Is it because you believe the way that you currently operate will be sufficient for the test of time?

Once you examine the change, list the pros and cons of the change. Be honest with yourself no matter how difficult it is. You have to be able to criticize yourself during this process so that you can see the light at the end of the tunnel.

Also, patience is a virtue during this time because you will not change overnight. It will take self-exploration, hard conversations with others, sleepless nights, and uncomfortable situations. However, this is all part of the process. It makes you a stronger person and leader, if that's what you desire to be. Be aware, this will take effort on your part; however through learning about yourself, you can be the example of change. If one person notices and decides they should follow your lead, the dominoes will fall and your personal and professional environment will grow into something you've always dreamed of. Stop making the excuse "that's the way you've always done it" and develop yourself through learning. When you make the aforementioned statement, you don't realize how narrow-minded you are in the grand scheme of the innovative world that we live in.

MISSION 1:

Examine one change that you're resisting in your personal or professional life and identify three reasons for your opposition.

MISSION 2

COME TOGETHER, KEEP TOGETHER, WORK TOGETHER

"Coming together is a beginning; keeping together is progress; working together is success."

—Henry Ford: American Industrialist and founder of the Ford Motor Company.

This sounds like Bruce Tuckman's Forming-Storming-Norming-Performing model from the mid 1960's. History indicates that this model works; however we continue to fight the process when it occurs. Think about this as it relates to a meeting or a brainstorming session. Many ideas are presented with discussions to follow. Discussions sometimes lead to arguments. These arguments then lead to an understanding. In any organization that has passionate people, this iterative process will occur. There's nothing wrong with this as long as it is kept professional. In the end, the group will be working together for the common goal. It takes those few minutes, hours, day, months, and in some cases, even years of uncomfortable conversations before everyone realizes that they are all on the same team.

Take that next meeting, discussion, brainstorming session, or whatever it may be as it is and let the process work. If we all told each other what we wanted to hear, we would never get anything accomplished and our ideas would be unimaginative. This doesn't create a competitive advantage or increase our service delivery. Be different and express ideas that need to be heard. Yes, the hard questions and discussions will ensue. However, if you can hang on for the ride, you'll learn lifelong lessons.

MISSION 2:

Rather than simply sit through a meeting or group discussion, get involved and present an idea that you're unsure of. You never know, others may also be thinking it but are afraid to take that step to the ledge and jump.

MISSION 3

CHANGE OR IRRELEVANCE, IT'S YOUR CHOICE

"If you don't like change, you will like irrelevance even less."

—GENERAL ERIC SHINESKI:
U.S. ARMY CHIEF OF STAFF 1999–2003.

Why do we fight change so much? If we think about it, change is really progress. This is a positive aspect of an organization that can increase its profit margin, but also enhance its customer service. Now granted, when we're first introduced to an organizational change, often times we think it won't work. Our mind is working against us in this situation with a process called negative filtering. During this process, we focus on negative aspects of a change, which in turn, makes us view the entire situation as negative. Simply put, we become so accustomed to the routines that we follow each day, the possibility of change makes us defensive and we then forget to look at the positives that may come from a new idea.

Now take a moment to think about irrelevance. Would you rather be the person driving the progress of your organization or the person no one wants to associate with? Eventually, the progress will come to fruition and if you're still the one withholding from the change, you'll become irrelevant in your workforce. It's a sad truth, but it's happened in organizations all over the world for decades.

Get on board with the change and realize that it's simply progress. This is essential for organizational improvement but also for your professional growth. Don't become irrelevant in the career that you've invested countless hours in. Take the changes head on and make a difference.

MISSION 3:

Review the three reasons you identified in Mission 1 for your resistance to change and then develop the plan to institute that change so you don't become irrelevant.

MISSION 4

WE MUST. . .

*"We must be silent before we can listen. We must
listen before we can learn. We must learn before
we can prepare. We must prepare before we can
serve. We must serve before we can lead."*

—WILLIAM ARTHUR WARD:
AMERICAN AUTHOR AND THEOLOGIAN.

Preparing to lead is a difficult process that starts long
before the first day in our career. It starts with silence.
Think about it. When we selected a profession and began
to learn new information, we were silent because the new
situation was intimidating. Once we started to understand key concepts, we were more attentive to detail.

After we learned the concepts and important aspects of the profession, we prepared ourselves for different organizational roles. This preparation made us more aware of the effort, patience, and commitment essential to serve and become a good follower. After all, we must be a good follower before we can step into a leadership role.

Finally, with the culmination of years of silence, listening, learning, preparing, and serving, the opportunity arises to lead and we feel we aren't ready. If you ask senior executives about their first leadership position, many will say they *thought* they were ready, but quickly realized that they had a great deal to learn. Key point here is that no matter how long we've been in our career, one hour or 50 years, leader or follower, we must learn every day. This may even mean that a colleague with less experience has more knowledge in a certain area. As a leader or a follower, we must put our ego aside and remember it doesn't matter who's right, it matters what's right. When we come together in this manner, the possibilities are endless.

MISSION 4:

Listen, learn, prepare, serve, and lead TOGETHER with a co-worker with whom you tend to have conflicting views. Challenge yourself during this mission and watch the growth occur. If you open up enough, you will have a new understanding of this person and their views.

MISSION 5

TIE A KNOT AND HANG ON

"When you reach the end of your rope,
tie a knot in it and hang on."

—FRANKLIN D. ROOSEVELT:
32ND PRESIDENT OF THE UNITED STATES.

Think about a time in your life where you thought you were at the end of your rope. Regardless if it's been in your personal or professional life, it's an extremely stressful time that challenges positive thinking. It's only a test. One more time. . . IT'S ONLY A TEST. Granted, this test wears us down and makes us question the road we've chosen. However, this test also sculpts us into who we are.

Take Thomas Edison for example. Researchers all over the world have debated how many times he failed before he finally created the light bulb. The estimations range from 1,000 to 10,000 attempts before he was successful at this life changing invention. Yes, he failed thousands of times before he figured out the right formula. However, he continued to try because he believed in himself and his work. When asked about his failures he stated, "I haven't failed; I've just found 10,000 ways that won't work."

Do you think he was at the end of his rope after thousands of unsuccessful attempts? Of course he was. Nevertheless, he continued to tie knots in that rope so he could hang on to his dream. He didn't feel sorry for himself. He kept trying as others laughed and ridiculed his work. Simply put, he was not afraid to fail as he knew success was imminent.

Granted, for some, success comes easy. However, for most of us, it takes tying a knot over and over again. Will you tie the necessary knots for success or cut the rope in fear of failure? Your personal and professional growth are waiting. Choose wisely.

MISSION 5:

Complete a personal or professional project that you've delayed for fear of failure. Whether it's lose 10 pounds, write a book, teach a class, volunteer, or whatever it may be. Finish that project!

MISSION 6

DO PEOPLE FEEL YOUR ATTITUDE?

"People may hear your words, but
they feel your attitude."

—John C. Maxwell:

AUTHOR, PASTOR, PROFESSIONAL SPEAKER.

Your attitude is a major component for success but also on the mark that you leave behind. Let's read that again. Your attitude is a major component for success but also on the mark that you leave behind. As history has indicated time and time again, it's very true.

In 1864, following a nitroglycerine accident that killed his brother Emil, an inventor named Alfred set out to develop a safer explosive. After years of research,

Alfred created the well-known explosive, dynamite. This made Alfred millions of dollars and allowed him to open more factories for production. Then in 1888, his brother Ludvig died. Alfred was devastated. He was then alarmed when he saw the obituary falsely indicating that HE, Alfred, had died, not Ludvig. Alfred now had the opportunity to read his epitaph while still being alive. It proclaimed that the "Tradesman of Death" was dead. This hurt Alfred.

Then in 1895, following years of thought on how to fix this perception, Alfred had a plan. He decided in his will that the predominance of his fortune would be specified for a yearly award that honored outstanding contributions for mankind. He wanted people to see his real attitude and remember him for something positive rather than as the merchant of death.

Today, Alfred Nobel is predominately known as the founder of the Nobel Peace Prize. He changed his attitude and the world will feel it forever. How will you be remembered personally and professionally? Will the people in your world feel it forever? Remember, attitude is a conscious decision that we have TOTAL control over.

MISSION 6:

Take stock in your current attitude, make the necessary adjustments, and watch the people around you feed off of your positivity. It's contagious. Spread it.

MISSION 7

DO SOMETHING REMARKABLE

*"What's the point of being alive if you don't
at least try to do something remarkable?"*

—Anonymous

Life is a beautiful gift full of ups and downs, successes and failures. This is a given that we should all be accustomed to from our experiences. However, some people do not function well when there is a time in their life that they are personally down or professionally failing. This creates a difficult environment for this person whether they are at home with their family, or at their place of employment with their colleagues.

With this being said, ask yourself: When trials and tribulations such as a change in my organization present themselves, do I become someone that resists the new change due to the fear of the unknown? Unfortunately, many of us will answer yes. The real question is, how long does this "yes" last for? Your answer will dictate if you're capable of something remarkable.

Take a look around your organization and identify the people that are becoming involved in the change process to ensure progression takes place. If you look closely enough, you will see individuals that are becoming more successful than they could have ever imagined. You may even be asking yourself why they are getting an opportunity for success when you feel it should be your opportunity. The problem does not lie within these individuals for embracing change. The problem lies within you.

Rather than wasting energy and telling everyone that they're drinking the proverbial Kool-Aid, pour yourself a glass and spend your time in a more purposeful manner. Sounds pretty simple, right? Well, it is. And it works.

MISSION 7:

Try the proverbial Kool-Aid and enjoy the positive energy that comes from it. Specifically, join in on a change initiative that you have resisted in the past. You never know, this may allow you to do something remarkable.

MISSION 8

WASTED TALENT?

*"The saddest thing in life is wasted talent and the
choices that you make will shape your life forever."*

—A Bronx Tale, 1993

What is your talent? Are you wasting it looking for an
easy way to get through each day or are you continually
looking to evolve? It's amazing how many talented people
are in this world but they hold themselves back by either
pure laziness, lack of ambition, or the fear that they will
fail. Living this way will not lead to a successful career or
a full personal life. One must utilize their talents to their
full potential or those talents become a waste; a waste not
only for the individual, but a waste for society as well.

Reflect on your high school and college years when there were individuals that had it all. They could play every sport, academics came easy, and everyone liked them. It seemed they had the world in their hands. It's funny when you see some of these individuals later in life and realize how much they wasted their talent because it all came so easy early on. Now granted, this doesn't happen to everyone; however, there are many times when this occurs.

Relate this to yourself in the present day. Are you comfortable with where you are in your life and don't feel that you need to improve upon anything? If you're not continually challenging yourself, then you need to identify why you're not continually challenging yourself. There are people in your profession and in your organization that are pushing the pace every day to be the best. Eventually, these people will be your boss and you will remain in that same comfortable position that you've had for years. This leads to reduced job satisfaction and resentment of co-workers. The comical part is that the resentment should be with yourself because you are the only one to blame for your lack of progression.

For example, in a public service organization, there was a secretary that was the assistant to the deputy chief. The deputy chief retired and a new one was promoted from within the ranks. The new deputy chief was very task oriented and focused on improving the organization. The secretary had worked for the former deputy chief for almost 10 years and did a great job for the first five or six years. However, after that, she became complacent in her position. The problem was that the former deputy chief did not say anything because he knew he was retiring soon.

During the first few weeks of the new deputy chief's tenure, he realized the secretary's lack of work production and that she was working on personal items during company time. He brought her in to his office to counsel her so she would improve. Following the meeting, she went directly to the head chief. She complained that the new deputy chief was being too hard on her and either he had to go or she did.

Now let's look at this situation. You have an individual that is not doing her job, wasting her talent, and inhibiting the organization from improving, yet, she feels that it's someone else's fault. This is not only sad but ridiculous. Here you have an adult that thinks it's acceptable to not do their work but then wants to blame it on someone else.

Have you ever done this? Have you wasted your talent over the years because you were busy focusing on other activities that were not important to your personal or professional improvement? Remember, your future is in your hands. You can waste your talent all you want, but don't blame others when the ambitious and focused professionals become leaders. It *will* eventually happen. So prepare yourself to say yes sir and yes ma'am to them. It's the least you can do for the hard work they performed and your lack of ambition that allowed them to pass you by.

MISSION 8:

Identify three activities that you perform during your day that are causing you to waste your talent. Once they're identified, delete them from your daily routine and replace them with new activities that are focused on every day dedication and improvement.

MISSION 9

HOW WINNING IS DONE

"The world ain't all sunshine and rainbows. It's a very mean and nasty place and I don't care how tough you are. It will beat you to your knees and keep you there permanently if you let it. You, me, or nobody is going to hit as hard as life. But it ain't about how hard you hit. It's about how hard you can get hit and keep moving forward. How much you can take and keep moving forward. That's how winning is done!"

—ROCKY BALBOA, 2006

One of the reasons why life is so beautiful is that you can do anything you want to do and be anything that you want to be. It doesn't matter how young or old you are.

If you have a dream, you must follow that dream with all of your efforts until you either achieve it or die trying. Now those are strong words, however, if you have true conviction in something, true faith, true belief; you must set out on that mission. Granted, you may not achieve that dream, but at least you can look yourself in the mirror and know that you gave it your all. No regrets. The problem is that people think they give it their all when in reality they're holding back due to fear or a lack of work ethic. They then blame others that are successful for their own shortfalls. Do you know people with this attitude? Hopefully, it's not you.

I'm going to give you a personal example in hopes that you can better relate to this type of situation. When I was growing up, all I ever wanted to do was play professional baseball. My dad threw me a baseball when I was 3 years old and for the next 21 years of my life, that's all I did. I chased my dream with every ounce of my being, every day, with all of my energy. Ask anyone that I played ball with and they will attest to this. I probably worked too hard, and at times, injured myself because I had no quit in my mind.

I played through high school, received a college scholarship, and played professionally. However, my professional career did not turn out like I had planned.

I didn't get drafted but I was fortunate enough to sign as a free agent with the independent Frontier League. My first year I did pretty well and again believed that I had a chance to move on to the next level. I worked extra every day to try and improve to the level of the athletes around me. I even told the manager I would try other positions just so I could continue to play. But at the end of it all, I wasn't good enough. Yes, that was a hard realization for me. I was a ball player for my entire life up to that point. I took pride in that. However, I look back at those times and don't blame anyone for me not making it to the big leagues. I chased my dream and failed. But at least I failed with no regrets and no fear.

I now watch major league baseball games and see a lot of people that I played ball with and against. It's so exciting to see that they achieved their dreams. I don't blame them because they made it and I didn't. They were better and deserved to make it. The problem is, I didn't always feel that way.

So, how did I come to this realization? I asked myself four hard questions while I stared in the mirror. I asked: "What is my dream? What am I doing to achieve that dream? Am I bitter with others that are more successful than me? Am I working hard enough to achieve my dream or am I waiting for someone to hand it to me on a silver platter?" Once I took the time to answer these hard questions, I had a new outlook. This allowed me to take ACTION.

Those four questions can do the same for you, if you're honest with yourself. Yes, they're going to test you emotionally. That's alright. Don't judge. Just answer the questions and let the self-exploration begin. Remember, you can either follow other people's dreams on social media and reality television as you make excuses or blame others OR you can challenge yourself and follow your own dreams. I'll let you decide which is considered winning. It shouldn't be too hard.

MISSION 9:

Find a mirror, look at yourself, and ask the following questions: "What is my dream? What am I doing to achieve my dream? Am I bitter with others that are more success-ful than me? Am I working hard enough to achieve my dream or am I waiting for some-one to hand it to me on a silver platter?"

EPILOGUE

This book was intended to provide an objective view of yourself, both personally and professionally. That's a very hard task to accomplish. It's frustrating, humbling, joyful, and disappointing at times. However, if we're not open to look at ourselves from this viewpoint, we'll go through life thinking that we're where we need to be. To me, this is the definition of complacency and that is something I can't live with nor will tolerate in my life.

As sports commentator and television personality Joe Rogan states, "Be the hero of your own movie." Think about that statement. Are you the hero of your own movie or are you just rolling through life hoping to fake it until you make it? There are many people that go through life in this manner and crazy enough, they make it to where they want to be. However, on the way there,